Your Government:
How It Works

The U.S.
Constitution

Joan Banks

Arthur M. Schlesinger, jr.
Senior Consulting Editor

Chelsea House Publishers
Philadelphia

CHELSEA HOUSE PUBLISHERS

Production Manager Pamela Loos
Art Director Sara Davis
Director of Photography Judy L. Hasday
Managing Editor James D. Gallagher
Senior Production Editor J. Christopher Higgins

Staff for THE U.S. CONSTITUTION

Project Editor/Publishing Coordinator Jim McAvoy
Associate Art Director Takeshi Takahashi
Series Designers Takeshi Takahashi, Keith Trego
Editorial Assistant Rob Quinn

First Printing
1 3 5 7 9 8 6 4 2

Library of Congress Cataloging-in-Publication Data

Banks, Joan, 1942–
     The U.S. Constitution / Joan Banks.
        p. cm.—(Your government—how it works)
     Includes bibliographical references and index.
     ISBN 0-7910-5991-X
     1. Constitutional history—United States.—Juvenile literature.
  2. Constitutional law—United States—Juvenile literature. 3. United
  States. Constitutional Convention (1787)—Juvenile literature.
  [1. Constitutional history—United States. 2. Constitutional law—
  United States. 3. United States. Constitutional Convention (1787)]
  I. Title: US CONSTITUTION. II Title. III. Series.

KF4541 .B3124 2000
342.73'029—dc21   00-034591

Contents

The Attorney General's Office

The Cabinet

The Central Intelligence Agency

The Drug Enforcement Administration

The Federal Bureau of Investigation

The History of the Democratic Party

The History of the Republican Party

The History of Third Parties

The House of Representatives

How a Bill Is Passed

How to Become an Elected Official

The Impeachment Process

The Internal Revenue Service

The Presidency

The Secretary of State

The Senate

The Speaker of the House of Representatives

The Supreme Court

The U.S. Armed Forces

The U.S. Constitution

The U.S. Secret Service

The Vice Presidency

Introduction

Government: Crises of Confidence

Arthur M. Schlesinger, jr.

FROM THE START, Americans have regarded their government with a mixture of reliance and mistrust. The men who founded the republic understood the importance of government. "If men were angels," observed the 51st Federalist Paper, "no government would be necessary." But men are not angels. Because human beings are subject to wicked as well as to noble impulses, government was deemed essential to assure freedom and order.

The American revolutionaries, however, also knew that government could become a source of injury and oppression. The men who gathered in Philadelphia in 1787 to write the Constitution therefore had two purposes in mind: They wanted to establish a strong central authority and to limit that central authority's capacity to abuse its power.

To prevent the abuse of power, the Founding Fathers wrote two basic principles into the Constitution. The principle of federalism divided power between the state governments and the central authority. The principle of the separation of powers subdivided the central authority itself into three branches—the executive, the legislative, and the judiciary—so that "each may be a check on the other."

YOUR GOVERNMENT: HOW IT WORKS examines some of the major parts of that central authority, the federal government. It explains how various officials, agencies, and departments operate and explores the political organizations that have grown up to serve the needs of government.

Introduction

The federal government as presented in the Constitution was more an idealistic construct than a practical administrative structure. It was barely functional when it came into being.

This was especially true of the executive branch. The Constitution did not describe the executive branch in any detail. After vesting executive power in the president, it assumed the existence of "executive departments" without specifying what these departments should be. Congress began defining their functions in 1789 by creating the Departments of State, Treasury, and War.

President Washington, assisted by Secretary of the Treasury Alexander Hamilton, equipped the infant republic with a working administrative structure. Congress also continued that process by creating more executive departments as they were needed.

Throughout the 19th century, the number of federal government workers increased at a consistently faster rate than did the population. Increasing concerns about the politicization of public service led to efforts—bitterly opposed by politicians—to reform it in the latter part of the century.

The 20th century saw considerable expansion of the federal establishment. More importantly, it saw growing impatience with bureaucracy in society as a whole.

The Great Depression during the 1930s confronted the nation with its greatest crisis since the Civil War. Under Franklin Roosevelt, the New Deal reshaped the federal government, assigning it a variety of new responsibilities and greatly expanding its regulatory functions. By 1940, the number of federal workers passed the 1 million mark.

Critics complained of big government and bureaucracy. Business owners resented federal regulation. Conservatives worried about the impact of paternalistic government on self-reliance, on community responsibility, and on economic and personal freedom.

When the United States entered World War II in 1941, government agencies focused their energies on supporting the war effort. By the end of World War II, federal civilian employment had risen to 3.8 million. With peace, the federal establishment declined to around 2 million in 1950. Then growth resumed, reaching 2.8 million by the 1980s.

A large part of this growth was the result of the national government assuming new functions such as: affirmative action in civil rights, environmental protection, and safety and health in the workplace.

Some critics became convinced that the national government was a steadily growing behemoth swallowing up the liberties of the people. The 1980s brought new intensity to the debate about government growth. Foes of Washington bureaucrats preferred local government, feeling it more responsive to popular needs.

But local government is characteristically the government of the locally powerful. Historically, the locally powerless have often won their human and constitutional rights by appealing to the national government. The national government has defended racial justice against local bigotry, upheld the Bill of Rights against local vigilantism, and protected natural resources from local greed. It has civilized industry and secured the rights of labor organizations. Had the states' rights creed prevailed, perhaps slavery would still exist in the United States.

Americans are still of two minds. When pollsters ask large, spacious questions—Do you think government has become too involved in your lives? Do you think government should stop regulating business?—a sizable majority opposes big government. But when asked specific questions about the practical work of government—Do you favor Social Security? Unemployment compensation? Medicare? Health and safety standards in factories? Environmental protection?—a sizable majority approves of intervention.

We do not like bureaucracy, but we cannot live without it. We need its genius for organizing the intricate details of our daily lives. Without bureaucracy, modern society would collapse. It would be impossible to run any of the large public and private organizations we depend on without bureaucracy's division of labor and hierarchy of authority. The challenge is to keep these necessary structures of our civilization flexible, efficient, and capable of innovation.

More than 200 years after the drafting of the Constitution, Americans still rely on government but also mistrust it. These attitudes continue to serve us well. What we mistrust, we are more likely to monitor. And government needs our constant attention if it is to avoid inefficiency, incompetence, and arbitrariness. Without our informed participation, it cannot serve us individually or help us as a people to attain the lofty goals of the Founding Fathers.

Delegates from all across the United States met at Independence Hall in Philadelphia to create a contract for uniting the 13 new states. The resulting Constitution of the United States has been the foundation for the longest-existing democracy in the history of the world.

CHAPTER 1

A Rising Sun

ON SEPTEMBER 17, 1787, four prisoners from the Philadelphia jail trundled down a brick street to the Pennsylvania State House, now called Independence Hall. Between them they carried a sedan chair, a box with windows supported on long poles. Inside sat Benjamin Franklin. Franklin suffered from a painful condition called gout and could barely walk, but in pain or not, he didn't want to miss this important day.

All through the long, hot summer he and other **delegates** had been working on a constitution to replace the **Articles** of Confederation of the United States. Now their work was almost done.

Other delegates were arriving. They represented 12 of the 13 United States. Only Rhode Island was not represented because it had refused to send delegates to this "Grand Convention" in the first place. One newspaper referred to the tiny state as "Rogue Island" and suggested it "be dropped out of the Union or [given] to the different States which surround her."

Benjamin Franklin was 81 years old when he signed his name upon the Constitution. Franklin had long served the country in a variety of endeavors, but it is said that signing the Constitution was his crowning moment.

The day had dawned cold and clear. Perhaps there were fires in the two fireplaces in the big room where the delegates met. Sunlight shone through the tall windows. This was the same room where the Declaration of Independence had been signed 11 years earlier, in 1776. Green cloths covered the tables in the room. Each table had an inkwell, so members could take notes with quill pens.

The prisoners parked the sedan chair at the back of the room and left, and Franklin went to sit with the other Pennsylvania delegates. The rest of them took their seats.

On the previous Saturday, the delegates had unanimously voted to accept this Constitution. After adjourning that day, a clerk, Jacob Shallus, was given the job of writing out a final copy of the document. Now the delegates listened to its words as it was read aloud. The ideas weren't new to them. All summer they had argued about this point or that. But now they heard all points presented in final form.

Benjamin Franklin rose. He had a speech prepared but was too weak to deliver it. He handed it to another man to read.

In the speech, Franklin said he didn't agree with everything in the Constitution they had written, but over his long life he'd learned that he wasn't always right. The speech ended by saying, "I consent, Sir, to this Constitution because I expect no better and because I am not sure that it is not the best."

Several other delegates spoke, then it was time for them to sign their names. The New Hampshire delegates went first. Then those from Massachusetts and Connecticut took their turns.

Alexander Hamilton was the only New York delegate present that day. He went forward and signed. He had missed some of the meetings, but like Franklin, this was one day he didn't want to miss. He had pushed for this sort of convention since 1780. He had a vision of America as a single nation, not a group of independent states.

Next came Pennsylvania. It had the most delegates at the convention, and all eight signed. Someone probably had to help Franklin go forward. It was said that tears welled in his eyes as he dipped his pen in the silver inkwell and wrote his name on the parchment before him.

He was 81 years old, the oldest delegate to the convention, and he had accomplished many things over the years. He had invented bifocal eyeglasses. Another invention, the lightning rod, protected buildings from "mischief from thunder and lightning." He had started a library and a city hospital. He had been a government representative from the young nation to France and had served as the head of his home state, Pennsylvania. He had signed the Declaration of Independence that changed the 13 colonies into 13 independent states, and he had signed the Treaty of Paris in 1783 that officially brought an end to the Revolutionary War. But this document before him was a crowning point of his long life.

Although Benjamin Franklin was the oldest man present that day, General George Washington of Virginia was probably the most respected. A few short years before, he had ably led the 13 colonies in their war for independence from England. As a general and now as a private citizen, this tall, quiet man inspired those around him. He had known for some time that the young nation needed a stronger central government. "Thirteen [states] pulling against each other . . . will soon bring ruin on the whole," he wrote. He'd had a bad year: his favorite brother had died, and Washington himself had been ill. He wanted to stay home at Mount Vernon. But his friends told him how important it was for him to be at the convention. Reluctantly, he came and was almost immediately put in charge. As president of the Constitutional Convention, his signature appeared above all the others on the Constitution.

Like Washington, James Madison had come to the convention as a delegate from Virginia. They were the only signers of the Constitution who later became U.S. presidents. Madison was a small man whose friends called him "Jemmy." When he spoke, people often had to ask him to speak louder. They wanted to hear what he had to say because his ideas were as big as he was small.

Madison would later be called the "Father of the Constitution" because the basic plan for the document came from him. During the meeting, he sat at a table and took

George Washington was probably the most respected man at the convention. As a sign of this respect, Washington's name appears above all others on the Constitution.

notes about everything that happened. "I was not absent a single day," he wrote, "nor more than a casual fraction of an hour in any day . . . " There were no tape recorders, video cameras, or word processors in those days, so Madison wrote his notes by hand, using abbreviations to keep up with the speakers. At night he copied his notes. He kept the notes private during his lifetime, but his will later gave

George Washington (right) watches over the Constitutional Convention as delegates add their names to the finished contract.

permission to make them public. The government paid his widow $30,000 for his papers, including *Notes of the Debates*. In 1840, they were published, and they still serve as the best record of what went on behind the closed doors of the Constitutional Convention.

Madison was probably disappointed that only three of the seven Virginia delegates signed the Constitution that day. Two were absent, and two were not happy with the document and chose not to sign.

To all of the men there, it had been a hard summer. They worked "six, and sometimes 7 hours sitting . . . " according to George Washington's diary. They had met six days a week. But they had done what they were sent there to do and more.

On went the procession of signers. Delaware's five delegates had signed. Then came North Carolina, South Carolina, and Georgia.

While the last representatives were signing, Franklin looked toward the chair where George Washington had sat during the convention. A sun was painted on its back. "I have often . . . looked at that . . . without being able to tell whether it was rising or setting," Franklin said, "But now at length I have the happiness to know that it is a rising and not a setting sun." It was his way of saying he had high hopes for the United States of America under the new Constitution.

CHAPTER 2

A Long Time Coming

THE "GRAND CONVENTION" or "Federal Convention," as the newspapers of the time called it, had been a long time coming. But the men at the convention were not writing the first agreement on self-government in the New World. In 1620, the Pilgrims who sailed to America on the *Mayflower* had signed a document that promised just and equal laws for the good of the people. It was called the Mayflower Compact.

For the next 150 years most of the newcomers to eastern North America were English, and they formed 13 British colonies. They were loyal to King George III, but they lived a long way from England. They had to govern themselves, and they grew to love their independence. Soon, though, their independence would be threatened.

For a long time, the British and the French had quarreled over what territory was whose in America. Both claimed some of the same land

THE DESTRUCTION OF TEA AT BOSTON HARBOR.

Unjust taxation was one of the main reasons that the American colonies chose to break away from England. The Boston Tea Party is one of the most famous examples of colonial protest against unfair taxes.

between the Appalachian Mountains and the Mississippi River. In 1754, the quarreling turned into a war called the French and Indian War.

After nine years of fighting, the British won the war. In winning, they gained more land and began to worry about how to protect its borders. They voted to put an army in the colonies and ordered the colonists to house and feed the soldiers. This didn't sit well with the colonists, and it was just the beginning.

There were war debts to pay, so the British government imposed a series of taxes on the colonies. One of these taxes was on tea. When a group of colonists dumped a load of tea into Boston Harbor to protest the tax, the government decided to punish the colonists. It passed what the colonists called "The Intolerable Acts." These acts gave more power to the British governor of Massachusetts, they closed the port of Boston, and they forced the Massachusetts colonists to house and feed British soldiers.

Delegates from 12 of the colonies met together in the First Continental Congress to talk about what they should do. They wanted to remain loyal to the king, but they also wanted the British government to repeal these "Intolerable Acts." The delegates voted not to trade with Great Britain until the acts were repealed.

Not only did the British refuse to repeal the acts, but the king also said the colonists should back down or be crushed. British troops moved in to seize military supplies in Massachusetts. When the colonists fought back, King George III declared war.

Again, delegates from each colony came together as one body to make plans for a continental army. They named George Washington commander in chief. Prior to that time, each of the colonies thought of itself as totally separate. The king's action united them.

On July 4, 1776, the Second Continental Congress adopted the Declaration of Independence. They were British colonies no more. They were states. The United States of America was born.

Before the war ended, each of the states had written its own constitution and had joined in a "league of friendship" with each other. Delegates were chosen to write the Articles of Confederation. This was the new country's first constitution. The Articles called for a congress to manage the country.

Congressmen were chosen for one-year terms and could not serve more than three out of every six years. One-year terms sounded good, but by the time a congressman learned his job, his term was over. It was not an efficient system.

In this system, the Congress elected a president. He did not head a separate branch of government. Congress was the *only* branch. The president was elected for a one-year term. In all, eight men served as "President of the

United States in Congress Assembled." The first president's name was John Hanson. One of the lasting things Hanson did was approve the Great Seal of the United States, which is still used today.

When the Revolutionary War ended, the young country faced one of the same problems the British had faced after the French and Indian War: war debts. How was the new nation going to pay them?

The colonists had purposely made the Articles of Confederation weak because they distrusted a strong national government. They hadn't given the national government the right to collect taxes. Congress had to ask the states for money and hope they would pay.

Rivalries sprang up between the states, and the Congress could do little to control them. It could not regulate trade between the states. Each state could print its own money and refuse to accept money from another state.

Perhaps worst of all, the Congress could only make changes in the Articles of Confederation when all the states agreed. Trying to get unanimous agreement was next to impossible. The states were like independent countries. People didn't consider themselves Americans. They called themselves by their state names, like Virginians or Pennsylvanians.

Many people were unhappy with the Confederation, and, in 1786, Massachusetts farmers proved just how dissatisfied people had become. Mobs of them marched on courthouses to protest the taxes that were causing them to lose their farms. Next, they marched on the state arsenal to seize guns and ammunition. State troops stopped what came to be called Shays' Rebellion (after the mob's leader Daniel Shays), but the riot scared people. If some people were this unhappy, they wondered, what was to keep such an uprising from happening again?

At about the same time, Virginia and Maryland were arguing about who could control navigation on the

In 1786, some Massachusetts farmers rebelled against taxes and were eventually stopped by the state's militia. Shays' Rebellion was one of the first signs that the Articles of Confederation weren't capable of supporting the country.

Potomac River. Several states sent delegates to Annapolis, Maryland, to settle the disagreement and discuss trade. James Madison and Alexander Hamilton were among the delegates. They had more than just trade on their minds.

They urged the group to recommend to Congress a general convention of all the states. Its purpose would be to rewrite the Articles of Confederation to make the document stronger.

Congress, with the disturbing Shays' Rebellion fresh in its mind, knew something had to be done to strengthen the country. In its weak condition, it could fall to an invasion by a foreign country. When the recommendation to call a convention came before it, Congress was ready.

So in May 1787, delegates began arriving in Philadelphia for a meeting; its purpose was to revise the Articles of Confederation.

The meeting was scheduled to begin on May 14, but roads were bad, and travel was slow. Some delegates didn't have the money to get there. On the appointed day, only delegates from Pennsylvania and Virginia had arrived. Delegates from the other states trickled into Philadelphia. It was May 25 before there was a **quorum.**

The first order of business was to choose someone to preside over the meeting. There was no question—George Washington was unanimously chosen.

There were no women or minorities present. In those days, custom did not allow women to take part in government, and African Americans and Native Americans were not citizens. It would be many years before these groups could participate fully in government.

Friends and relatives prodded the delegates for news about what was happening behind the closed doors of the Convention. But from the start, the delegates agreed that what happened had to be kept secret until they had finished their work. They wanted to be able to speak freely. To make sure people did not eavesdrop, guards were posted at the door, and the blinds were drawn. James Madison's father wrote him a letter complaining that if James could not tell him what they were doing, could he at least tell him what they were *not* doing?

One day a delegate dropped his notes as he was leaving the hall. The following day, George Washington scolded them all and reminded them they must be more careful so the newspapers would not find out what was going on.

On Tuesday, May 29, the governor of Virginia, Edmund Randolph, stood up to speak. Many of the delegates powdered their hair to make it look white, but Randolph wore his dark hair loose and unpowdered. His brown eyes flashed when he spoke.

While they'd been waiting for the other delegates to arrive in Philadelphia, Randolph, Madison, and the other delegates from Virginia had spent their mornings putting together a plan. They thought it would give the Convention some direction. Many people believe that the plan was largely the work of James Madison. He had read many books about earlier confederations and democracies, and now all he had learned was coming together. He was especially influenced by the work of a French philosopher called Montesquieu, who believed that law underlies all things. Montesquieu also thought political freedom required separating the powers of government into three branches: legislative (Congress), judicial (the courts) and executive (the president). This idea was part of the so-called Virginia Plan and later became part of the U.S. Constitution.

Under the Virginia Plan, the legislative branch of the government would be bicameral, or divided into two chambers. The people would elect members of the first chamber. The number of members in the first chamber would depend upon the number of people living in a state. The members of the second chamber would be chosen by those in the first. The Virginia Plan suggested one executive as leader of the country, but the plan didn't use the word *president*. That term would come later in the Convention.

As Edmund Randolph revealed the Virginia Plan, some of the members were surprised. They had come to Philadelphia expecting to revise the Articles of Confederation, but this Virginia Plan went much farther. It was proposing a new plan of government.

James Madison is considered by many to be the father of the Constitution. Many of the ideas found in the Constitution were proposed by Madison. He later became the fourth president of the United States.

CHAPTER 3

Compromises Great and Small

BY THE TIME EDMUND Randolph sat down, the delegates were shocked into silence. He had not only proposed a new plan of government, but he had used the word *national*. Today, the words *federal* and *national* are used to mean the same thing. But in 1787, a federal government meant one in which the states were the most powerful. It is what the states had under the Articles of Confederation. But a national government took the main power from the states and gave it to the nation. The nation's interests would overrule the individual states. The very idea frightened many of the delegates.

The next days at the convention were filled with debate over the Virginia Plan. It favored the large states, said some of the delegates. Then William Paterson of New Jersey put a new plan before the convention. His New Jersey Plan suggested that the convention stick with what they had been sent there to do: revise the Articles of

Confederation. It proposed a system which kept power at the state level. It proposed having only one legislative body. In that body, each state's votes would be equal. The New Jersey Plan also proposed having more than one executive.

Some of the delegates liked the New Jersey Plan. They wanted the states to control the national government, not the other way around.

But James Wilson of Pennsylvania asked, "Why should a national government be unpopular? . . . Will a citizen of *Delaware* be degraded by becoming a citizen of the *United States*?"

Now Alexander Hamilton took the floor. He had served as General Washington's aide during the Revolutionary War. He was only five foot seven, and his nickname was "The Little Lion." He announced that he had a third plan in mind. He wanted to have America in the hands of a single executive who would be chosen for life by electors and would have an absolute **veto.** Most of the delegates probably frowned at his words. A single executive for life made them think of a king, and King George III of England was too fresh in their minds. This idea of Hamilton's was seen as outrageous.

Hamilton went on to say his vision of the government would have two chambers. The members of the upper chamber would be chosen for life. The lower chamber would be elected by the people and would be a balance on the power of the upper house. State governors would be appointed by the national government.

He spoke for six hours that day, but the length of his speech made no difference. The supporters of both the Virginia Plan and the New Jersey Plan rejected Hamilton's view. It went too far. Some people think he suggested such a plan to make the Virginia Plan seem more acceptable.

There was no air-conditioning in those days, and the room grew hot as the day went on. The delegates wore

Alexander Hamilton supported the idea of a strong central government. He made some suggestions at the convention that many delegates thought went too far. Some people think he only suggested those ideas to make the other plans seem more acceptable.

suits, probably made of wool. Some may have worn vests as well. Breeches and stockings covered their legs. They adjourned by three o'clock to get out of the stifling heat.

The next day, Madison was ready to fly into the New Jersey Plan. He didn't so much as mention Hamilton's plan. When the states took a vote that day, they sided with Madison for the Virginia Plan, seven to three.

Now the delegates needed to fine-tune the Virginia Plan. Little by little, they did so. They decided on issues such as who would be at the head of the government. How long would the executive's term be? What would the executive be called? There were dozens and dozens of issues to think about as they invented a government. Most of the delegates had experience in their own state bodies to draw upon.

Debate heated up again as they discussed how many representatives each state was to have in the legislature. The delegates came back to this question time and time again. It was one of the most difficult decisions of the convention. The large states of Virginia, Pennsylvania, and Massachusetts wanted representation in the first chamber of the legislature to be according to population. The states with small populations preferred equal representation. The southern states wanted to count their slaves as part of the population, so they would have more representatives.

The weather was hot, and tempers were, too. Finally, the delegates agreed that population of the states would be based on the white inhabitants and three-fifths of the "other people." It did not use the word *slaves*. This was called the "three-fifths **compromise.**" The delegates went on to agree that representation in the first chamber would be based on population. In the second chamber, there would be equal representation, no matter what the population. This concept became known as "The Great Compromise." Each side gave in a little so the convention could once again move forward.

The hot spell in Philadelphia broke, and a committee was given the task of drawing up a first draft of the Constitution. The other members took a much-needed 10-day vacation. George Washington and Gouverneur Morris of Pennsylvania rode out to Valley Forge. Ten years earlier Washington had spent a winter here with his freezing troops during the Revolutionary War. He may have thought about how far the country had come from that time when the outcome of the war was so uncertain, to this hot

summer when he and other leaders were making plans for a new constitution.

The delegates came back together on August 6. There were more details to work out. When should the legislature meet? How long must a foreign-born person live in the country before being eligible to be in Congress? Where would the government be? The Congress of the Confederation had moved from city to city. All of the delegates felt this weakened the government, but they left the location open. It would be for the new Congress to decide.

By the end of the month another major compromise had been made. It was about slavery. Some delegates wanted to end slave selling. After all, they said, if the Constitution stood for liberty, how could it allow slavery? George Mason of Virginia, who owned 200 slaves, said, "I hold it essential . . . that the general government should have power to prevent the increase of slavery . . . " Others thought it was no business of the Constitution whether

Washington's return visit to Valley Forge must have brought back memories of the winter he'd spent there with the Continental army during the Revolutionary War.

Slavery was wide-spread in the United States while the Constitution was being drafted. Many delegates wanted to abolish the slave trade, but they failed to bring an end to slavery in the United States at that time.

people owned slaves or not. Their job, they said, was not to make new laws but rather to reflect the country as it was. The two sides finally compromised again. They agreed that the government would not stop slaves from being brought into the country until 1808. Unfortunately, the provision was not well enforced. Slaves continued to be imported after that date.

The delegates argued again about how to choose the executive. The Virginia Plan had proposed that the executive be chosen by the legislature. But many delegates felt that would give the legislature too much power over the executive. Gouverneur Morris of Pennsylvania suggested the executive be elected directly by the people. Roger Sherman of Connecticut thought that was an awful idea. He didn't think the people could ever get behind one candidate. Each state would have its favorite one, and the votes would be hopelessly divided.

A rumor spread that the convention was going to ask one of King George's sons to be the king of America. The delegates promptly sent a letter to a newspaper saying,

". . . tho' we cannot affirmatively tell you what we are doing, we can, negatively, tell you what we are not doing—we never once thought of a king."

They voted 60 times before they could agree on how to choose an executive. They finally compromised with a process called the electoral college. It satisfied those delegates who didn't want the executive to be chosen by the legislature, and it also pleased those who didn't believe the people knew enough to choose a good leader.

The electoral college provided that people of each state would choose electors, who would meet and vote for the president and vice president. If there were a tie, the first chamber of the national government would vote on the candidates with the largest number of votes. This system satisfied a majority of the delegates. Another decision had been made.

Then the delegates appointed a committee to put the finishing details on the Constitution, and on September 17, 1787, it was time to sign.

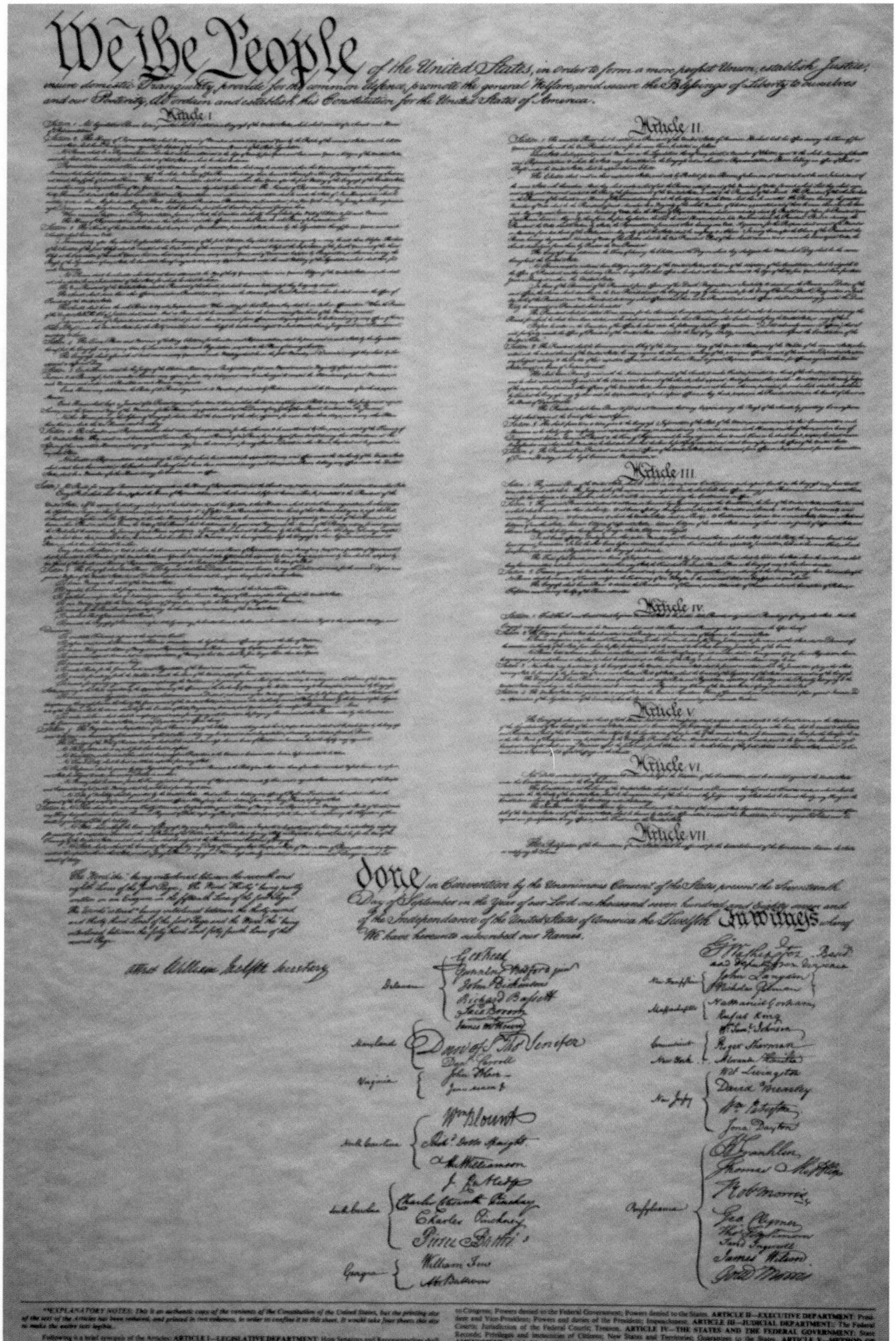

We the People

of the United States, in Order to form a more perfect Union, establish Justice, insure domestic Tranquility, provide for the common defence, promote the general Welfare, and secure the Blessings of Liberty to ourselves and our Posterity, do ordain and establish this Constitution for the United States of America.

Article I

Article II

Article III

Article IV

Article V

Article VI

Article VII

done in Convention by the Unanimous Consent of the States present the Seventeenth Day of September in the Year of our Lord one thousand seven hundred and Eighty seven and of the Independence of the United States of America the Twelfth In witness whereof We have hereunto subscribed our Names.

attest William Jackson Secretary

*EXPLANATORY NOTES: This is an authentic copy of the contents of the Constitution of the United States, but the printing size of the text of the Articles has been reduced, and printed in two columns, in order to confine it to this sheet. It would take four sheets this size to make the entire text legible.

Following is a brief synopsis of the Articles: **ARTICLE I—LEGISLATIVE DEPARTMENT**: How Senators and Representatives shall be chosen, and when they are to meet; Rules of procedure, compensation, privileges and restrictions; Mode of passing laws; Powers granted to Congress; Powers denied to the Federal Government; Powers denied to the States. **ARTICLE II—EXECUTIVE DEPARTMENT**: President and Vice-President; Powers and duties of the President; Impeachment. **ARTICLE III—JUDICIAL DEPARTMENT**: The Federal Courts; Jurisdiction of the Federal Courts; Treason. **ARTICLE IV—THE STATES AND THE FEDERAL GOVERNMENT**: State Records; Privileges and immunities of Citizens; New States and Territories; Guarantees to the States. **ARTICLE V—METHOD OF AMENDMENT. Article VI—PUBLIC DEBT; SUPREMACY OF THE CONSTITUTION; OATH OF OFFICE**; no religious test required. **ARTICLE VII—RATIFICATION OF THE CONSTITUTION.**

Even though the Constitution was completed and signed, it still faced many obstacles. In order for it to become law, nine states would have to vote to abide by the document and its principles.

CHAPTER 4

The Rocky Road to Ratification

BENJAMIN FRANKLIN WROTE TO his sister and told her that the work had been difficult and that perhaps everyone wouldn't receive it well. "We have, however, done our best, and it must take its chance."

After the signing, the delegates held a farewell dinner at City Tavern. While they ate, printers went to work to set the type and print a copy of the Constitution. The following morning, the document was sent by stagecoach to New York City, where the Congress of the Confederation was meeting.

Eight days after receiving the document, the Congress recommended that the states call conventions to **ratify** the new Constitution. The Constitution itself required nine states to ratify before the document would become legal.

The secrecy of the Federal, or Constitutional, Convention was over, and the document was made public. Across the young country, people picked up their newspapers and read:

We the People of the United States, in Order to form a more perfect Union, establish Justice, insure domestic Tranquility, provide for the common defence, promote the general Welfare, and secure the Blessings of Liberty to ourselves and our Posterity, do ordain and establish this Constitution for the United States of America.

This **preamble** was followed by a document made up of seven articles, or sections. The first three articles dealt with the legislative, the executive, and the judicial branches of the government. Each had separate powers. The legislative branch, the Congress, would make the laws. It would have two branches: a House of Representatives and a Senate. The executive branch, headed by the president, would carry out the laws Congress made, and the judicial branch would make sure the laws were constitutional. The judicial branch would have a Supreme Court at its head.

Each branch would serve as a check on the others. For instance, if Congress passed a law the president didn't like, the president could veto it. Congress could override his veto by a two-thirds majority vote. Supreme Court justices were to be appointed by the president, but his appointments had to be approved by Congress. The Congress could remove both the president and the justices from office if necessary.

Article IV of the Constitution defined the way states were to work with each other. It also guaranteed that the states would have representative forms of government and that the national government would protect the states against invasion.

Article V spelled out how the Constitution could be amended, or changed. The Articles of Confederation had been almost impossible to change because all of the states had to agree. The new Constitution only required agreement by three-fourths of the states.

Article VI affirmed that the Constitution was to be the supreme law of the land and that officials of the govern-

The Constitution established the three branches of government as a balance of power. The Supreme Court is head of the judicial branch.

ment were to give it the utmost loyalty. It also said that people couldn't be kept from holding office because of their religious beliefs. Since some colonists had fled from other countries to escape being punished for their religious beliefs, this was an important clause to them.

People were puzzled by what they read. They discussed it with their friends. They went to taverns and meeting houses and discussed what they had read. Some probably couldn't decide if they liked this new Constitution. It was a lot to think about. After all, some of the best minds in the country had drawn it up, and it had taken them all summer to write it. Other people probably made up their minds quickly.

The people who supported the Constitution and a strong national government were called **Federalists.** The people against the Constitution were **Anti-Federalists**— though they said they were the true Federalists.

A series of newspaper essays that began in October 1787 gave the Federalist, or pro-Constitution, position. It was the custom of the time to write essays under a pen name (false name used by an author), and these were written under the name *Publius.* Actually, three men wrote them: Alexander Hamilton, James Madison, and John Jay. Not everyone read the essays at the time they were written, but *The Federalist,* as the group of essays have come to be called, has lived on as the best explanation of the United States Constitution.

The arguments of the Federalists were well thought out. Many of the Federalists had been thinking about a document like the Constitution for a long time. Some had attended the Constitutional Convention and had already worked through any doubts they had.

The Anti-Federalists, on the other hand, were not as organized. William R. Davie, who had been a delegate to the Constitutional Convention from North Carolina, said, "It is much easier to alarm people than to inform them." His words summed up what many Anti-Federalists tried to do. They often used language to scare people. One man said that the "Federal City" called for in the Constitution would be walled in and have perhaps 100,000 men who would go forth and enslave the people. Another Anti-Federalist pictured tax collectors with bayonets and swords. Some people objected because they feared losing power in their own states. Others feared that a strong national government would work against state interests.

Not all Anti-Federalists based their arguments on emotion. Some had logical reasons to oppose a strong national government. Many agreed with George Mason, one of the Virginia delegates who had refused to sign the Constitution. He objected to it because it was mainly a plan of government. It guaranteed few individual rights. He had written the Virginia Declaration of Rights in 1776, and he felt the new Constitution needed such a declaration, too.

The day after the convention adjourned, the Constitution was read to the Pennsylvania legislature, which was sitting in the Pennsylvania State House, where the document had been signed the day before. George Clymer, who had been a delegate to the convention, proposed that the legislature call a state convention for ratification.

Anti-Federalists in the legislature were against moving so fast. To block the matter, these men didn't show up at the state house when the vote was scheduled. Their absence left the legislature without a quorum. A man was sent out to find them. He found them locked in their lodgings.

A mob went to the rooming house and reportedly hurled rocks through the windows. Two of the Anti-Federalists were dragged out and forced to go to the state house. Spectators actually applauded and laughed. It was all very undignified.

Now that it had a quorum, the Pennsylvania legislature voted to hold a ratification convention. It met for five weeks. James Wilson, who had signed the Constitution, told members about the long debates of the summer, and Pennsylvania appeared to be on its way to being the first state to ratify.

Meanwhile, with much less chaos, Delaware held its ratifying convention. On December 6, its vote gained it the distinction of becoming the first state under the new Constitution. Delaware was one of only three states that ratified unanimously. All delegates in Delaware, New Jersey, and Georgia voted for ratification.

Six days after Delaware, Pennsylvania ratified, with 46 yeas and 23 nays, making it the second state under the Constitution. But the vote wasn't the end of Anti-Federalist anger in the state. At a rally celebrating the Constitution, Anti-Federalists attacked James Wilson, who had explained the Constitution so well at the state convention. He was beaten with clubs and might have died if another man had not thrown himself between

Wilson and his attackers, according to one report. Upon hearing news of the ratification, a mob in one Pennsylvania town burned an **effigy** of Wilson and a copy of the Constitution.

New Jersey, Georgia, and Connecticut ratified after Pennsylvania, in that order. Five states had now ratified. The Constitution directed that, for it to become the supreme law of the land, nine states must ratify it. Which would be next?

The Massachusetts Convention ratified on February 6, 1788. It directed its future representatives to work toward **amendments** to the Constitution. The Massachusetts representatives wanted the same sort of guarantees that George Mason had in mind. But other delegates to the convention, like Alexander Hamilton and James Madison, had not thought a "bill of rights" was necessary. Hamilton thought that listing basic rights would make people think rights not listed did not exist. Madison believed the Constitution already protected citizens' rights against the tyranny of the central government by separating its powers into three branches.

Madison had been in New York working with Alexander Hamilton on the essays of *The Federalist,* but in March 1788, he returned to his home in Virginia. In June he attended the Virginia Ratification Convention.

Madison's opponent at the convention was Patrick Henry. He was the Virginian who had urged his fellow Virginians to take up arms against the British with the famous words: " . . . give me liberty or give me death." The tall and fiery Henry hadn't attended the Constitutional Convention in Philadelphia because he said he smelled a rat. He suspected that the purpose of the convention was to create a strong national government. His suspicions were right. And now he had plenty to say about this proposed Constitution. To him, *it* was the rat.

Patrick Henry was a fiery politician from Virginia. He had often spoken out against British rule, and he argued that the Constitution took too much power from the states.

Patrick Henry disliked the opening words of the Constitution's preamble. "Who authorizes gentlemen to speak the language of We, the people, instead of We, the states? . . . The people gave them no power to use their name." He accused the supporters of the Constitution of playing on the fears of what would happen if the states didn't ratify it.

Henry had been a strong power in state politics and could probably see his power slipping away if the power of the states was weakened by a national government.

On the other side, James Madison took the floor and called on the delegates' intelligence, saying that they must "examine the Constitution on its own merits."

The Virginia Convention went through the Constitution bit by bit. Arguments arose, and it was tiresome for Madison. He had been through all this before in Philadelphia. Now he was going through it again.

At the convention in Philadelphia, Edmund Randolph, who had presented the Virginia Plan, surprised his fellow delegates when he refused to sign the Constitution. After all, the Virginia Plan had formed the Constitution's backbone.

Now he stepped before his fellow Virginians at their ratification convention. They probably thought he would be against ratification. But then he surprised them. He said if he were back at the Philadelphia Convention, he would still refuse to sign. He said he couldn't at that time sign the Constitution without the addition of a bill of rights. But now, he told them, Massachusetts had ratified with an urging that certain amendments be added. He thought Virginia should do the same thing because there was no time to waste. To not ratify, he said, would bring ruin to the nation.

Patrick Henry made fun of Randolph's change of heart. His comments implied that George Washington had influenced Randolph's opinion. This made Randolph angry. He said, "If our friendship fall, let it fall . . . never to rise again. . . . Sir, if I do not stand on the bottom of integrity and pure love for Virginia as much as those who can be most clamorous, I wish to resign my existence."

Meanwhile, Maryland and South Carolina had ratified. When New Hampshire ratified on June 21, 1788, it became the ninth state to do so. Its ratification turned the Constitutional Convention's plan into reality: a new government was to be formed.

Four days later, Virginia ratified. This gave the document enough support to become official. Like Massachusetts, Virginia recommended a bill of rights be added to the document.

Now it was time to celebrate!

Philadelphia had its celebration on the fourth of July. At sunrise, bells rang out from the churches, and a cannon was shot. Ships were decorated; flags flew. The city staged a huge parade. It seemed that everyone, from bricklayers to goldsmiths to bakers to soldiers, took part.

There was a float depicting a ship called the Union. The sight of the ship brought on a "solemn silence," according to Dr. Benjamin Rush, who had signed the Declaration of Independence. The people seemed awed. "We have become a nation," Rush wrote.

With the Constitution ratified, the newly formed government had to be organized. Following the first elections, George Washington became the nation's first president and was sworn in April 30th, 1789.

CHAPTER 5

A Long Shadow

NEW YORK'S RATIFICATION on July 26, 1788, meant that all the states but two, North Carolina and Rhode Island, had ratified the Constitution. But it took some time for the wheels of government to start turning anew. There were senators and representatives to choose. There was the organization of the House of Representatives and the Senate to attend to. Electors had to be chosen so that they could elect a president. There was an executive branch to create.

"We are in a wilderness without a single footstep to guide us," said newly elected representative James Madison.

In Virginia, Madison's name had been put forward as a candidate for the United States Senate. But the Constitution, before it was changed by the Seventeenth Amendment, gave the state legislature the right to choose the two senators. The Virginia legislature was controlled by the Anti-Federalist Patrick Henry, so it was no surprise when two Anti-Federalists were elected.

Madison decided to run for the House of Representatives. He ran against another future president, James Monroe. The campaign was friendly. The two even traveled together when they were campaigning. The worst of the campaign came one cold night when Madison's nose was frostbitten; the best came when he won the election.

The First Congress of the United States was scheduled to begin meeting on March 4, 1789, but like the Constitutional Convention, it had trouble getting a quorum. Winter weather and bad roads had kept many congressmen away, and it wasn't until April 1 that enough members had arrived to conduct business in the House of Representatives. The Senate achieved a quorum a few days later.

The first order of business was to find out who was going to be the first president, although everyone was certain it would be George Washington. The two chambers came together to count the electoral votes, which had been cast in February by the electoral college. Electors had each cast two votes—one for president and one for vice president. As was expected, each elector had given one of his votes to Washington, making his election as president unanimous. The electors' second votes were divided among a field of candidates, but John Adams won the most votes and became the first vice president. Adams, who had signed the Declaration of Independence, had been a minister to Great Britain during the convention. Otherwise his name would have probably been on the Constitution as well.

On April 30, 1789, Washington, dressed in a dark brown suit, white silk stockings, and black shoes with silver buckles, stood before his countrymen and placed his hand on a Bible and repeated the oath of office, as written in Article II of the Constitution.

Then the man who administered the oath turned to the crowd and shouted: "Long live George Washington, President of the United States!" The crowd joined the cheer.

Now the country was truly in motion. Washington felt a heavy responsibility. Everything he did would set a pattern for the presidents who followed him.

The Congress had the same sense of duty. The way they chose to conduct the legislature would cast a long shadow over future legislatures.

One thing Madison had learned while campaigning for Congress was how important a bill of rights was to the people of Virginia. Now Congressman Madison's first order of business was to introduce such a bill. In some ways, he feared doing so. He worried that people would violate it and that the government might not be strong enough to do anything about it. Unpunished violations would weaken the Constitution and the government. He had seen this happen in Virginia.

His friend Thomas Jefferson, author of the Declaration of Independence and a minister to France during the Constitutional Convention, was in favor of a bill of rights. It was "what the people are entitled to against every government on earth . . . and what no just government should refuse . . . ," he wrote from Paris. Perhaps Jefferson's opinion made Madison feel better about introducing a bill of rights. Madison also thought it would encourage the remaining states, North Carolina and Rhode Island, to hold ratifying conventions.

So just days after Washington's inauguration, Madison brought the subject of a bill of rights before Congress. Many of the newly appointed representatives weren't ready to consider such a bill just then. First things first, they said. They wanted to wait until they had the government running smoothly. Some representatives wanted to wait a year. Others said that their states had ratified the Constitution without a bill of rights, and that was the way they wanted it to stay.

But Madison and his bill of rights weren't going away. In June, he brought the subject up again.

Thomas Jefferson favored a bill of rights. It was his opinion that people were entitled to such a bill to protect against an unfair government.

One proposal forbade Congress from making laws that would take away basic rights like freedom of religion, freedom of the press, freedom of speech, and the right to peaceably assemble.

Congressman Sedgewick of Massachusetts protested about adding the "right to peaceably assemble." If people have the right to get together and talk, he said, then it's unnecessary to give them the right to peaceably assemble. One can't be done without the other. Perhaps, he added sarcastically, the committee should add that a man has a right to wear a hat and that he has a right to get up and go to bed when he pleases.

These children are exercising their right to peaceably assemble in order to protest for the need for more recycling. James Madison wanted to create a bill of rights which would guarantee freedoms, such as this one, for all people.

Sedgewick need not have worried. James Madison had that covered by another of his proposals. It said that listing certain rights in the Constitution does not mean that the people do not have other rights.

Other proposals addressed the security of the people. The Revolutionary War was fresh in the congressmen's minds. They remembered how the British had forced the colonists to house and feed soldiers. They never wanted a government to do that to them again without their consent. They also wanted the right to have a state militia that could arm itself against a tyrannical government like the one they had known under the British.

It seemed there was something for everyone to complain about. One proposal forbade cruel and unusual punishment. A congressman stood up and spoke. "It is sometimes necessary to hang a man," he said. "Villains often deserve whipping, and perhaps having their ears cut off, but are we in [the] future to be prevented from inflicting these punishments because they are cruel?" His words did not keep the proposal from being included.

The discussion went on, with congressmen questioning this wording and that idea. Some proposals protected people's rights in court. One said that powers not given to the United States were reserved for the people or the states.

So far, the proposals told what the federal government could not do. The next proposal was aimed at the states. It said they could not take away certain rights protected by the U.S. Constitution. Madison thought this was the most important of all the proposals, but he knew how strongly people felt about states' versus national rights. He probably held his breath, expecting a long debate. He had been through the debates about states' rights at the Constitutional Convention and in the Virginia Ratification Convention. But to his surprise, the House of Representatives accepted the clause with little discussion.

But his relief came too early. When this proposal went to the Senate for approval, it failed to pass. Only after a deadly **civil war** (1861–1865) did Americans receive a guarantee that the states would not infringe upon the rights given them by the U.S. Constitution and its amendments. This guarantee became the 14th Amendment to the Constitution, ratified on July 9, 1868.

In all, the Senate proposed 12 amendments to the state legislatures for ratification as a bill of rights. Madison had condensed 27 rights for individuals into eight of these amendments.

Three-fourths of the states had to ratify the amendments for them to become law. Virginia's approval on

December 15, 1791, made 10 of the 12 proposed amendments part of the Constitution. They are called the Bill of Rights. Massachusetts, which had originally called for a bill of rights, never did ratify, nor did Georgia or Connecticut.

The states had only ratified 10 of the proposed amendments, but no time limit was placed on ratifying the other two. And so it was that over 200 years later in 1992, Michigan became the 38th state to ratify the second proposed amendment. It became part of the Constitution as the 27th Amendment. It says that an election must occur before a congressional pay raise can take effect. This gives voters a chance to vote a person out of office for increasing his or her own salary. The first proposed amendment has never been ratified. It dealt with the size of the House of Representatives.

The Virginia Declaration of Rights, which Madison had looked to as a guide in writing his proposals, had used such words as *ought not* and *should not.* The amendments to the U.S. Constitution weren't so cautious. They said, "Congress *shall* make no law . . . " and "the right . . . *shall not* be violated." The meaning couldn't have been stronger. The Bill of Rights guaranteed that the United States government would not take away the basic rights of its citizens.

CHAPTER 6

A Flexible Fit

"I NEVER EXPECT TO see a perfect work from imperfect man," Alexander Hamilton wrote in the last of *The Federalist* essays. He was writing about the Constitution. Perhaps it was not perfect, but striving to make it *more* perfect began almost immediately after ratification and has never stopped. People still argue about what various parts of it mean. It has been left to the Supreme Court to decide.

In 1803, the Supreme Court established its right to overturn laws that Congress passed in the case of *Marbury v. Madison*. On his last day in office, President John Adams appointed William Marbury as a justice of the peace, but the official papers were never delivered to Marbury. Almost 10 months later, Marbury asked the Supreme Court to order James Madison, by then the secretary of state for President Thomas Jefferson, to deliver the papers. Usually the Supreme Court was a court of last resort, which meant it heard cases **appealed** to it from a lower court. But Marbury had come directly to the Supreme Court with his request because of a law that Congress had passed in 1789. One of its clauses stated that the Supreme Court could order federal officials to perform their duties.

The Supreme Court threw Marbury's case out, not because it didn't want Marbury to be a justice of the peace, but because the Court said Congress had passed an unconstitutional law. The Supreme Court "checked" the power of Congress, making sure that Congress didn't become too powerful.

"It is . . . the province and duty of the judicial department to say what the law is," wrote Chief Justice of the Supreme Court John Marshall.

In 1833, the Supreme Court made another ruling that would have long-lasting effects. The Court was meeting in a room described by the *New York Tribune* as "a potato hole of a place . . . of small dimensions and shaped overhead like a quarter section of a pumpkin shell." It was in a basement in the rather new federal city of Washington, D.C., which was itself a dusty or muddy place, depending on the weather. Farm animals roamed through its streets. It did not seem like a capital city, and that basement room did not seem like a place for supreme justice to be carried out.

But supreme justice is what a man named John Barron hoped for when his case came before the Court. Barron said that the city of Baltimore had ruined his profitable business. The muddy run-off from the city's building projects had turned the once deep harbor at his dock into a shallow body of water where ships couldn't dock. Barron felt the Fifth Amendment should protect him. It states that a person should not "be deprived of life, liberty, or property, without due process of law; nor shall private property be taken for public use without just compensation."

After hearing the evidence, the Supreme Court ruled that the Fifth Amendment did not apply to the states. Chief Justice Marshall wrote, "The constitution was ordained and established by the people of the United States for themselves, for their own government, and not for the government of the individual states."

His words meant that the Bill of Rights only guaranteed that the *national* government would not violate people's rights. It did not guarantee that a state would not do so. A state could pass a law that denied a person the right to free speech, or it could shut down the newspapers. According to Marshall, it was none of the federal government's business. James Madison had worried about this problem when he first proposed the Bill of Rights to Congress, but the Senate had rejected the amendment that would have forbade the states from **infringing** upon the rights guaranteed by the Constitution. Fortunately, state constitutions provided some protections. The question of states' rights kept coming up.

Nowhere was the question stronger than between the North and the South. The two parts of the country were very different, and both had special interests they wanted to protect. The South depended mainly on agricultural crops, cotton, tobacco, and sugar. It exported most of these to Europe. Almost one-third of all Southern families owned slaves to help on their farms and plantations. It was unthinkable to the South that slavery might be abolished. It not only furnished the labor for their plantations, but it was part of their way of life. The North depended more upon industry.

Neither side wanted the other to get more votes in the Senate. The Southerners worried that if most of the senators were antislavery, slavery would be outlawed. The Northerners didn't want the Southerners to extend slavery. It was like a tug-of-war every time a new state or territory

A slave named Dred Scott attempted to gain his freedom by taking his case to the Supreme Court. The Court would not hear his case because, at the time, blacks were not considered citizens of the United States.

was added to the Union. Each side didn't want the other side to get ahead. Adding to the tension between the North and the South was another case that came before the Supreme Court.

In about 1832 a slave called Dred Scott was sold to Dr. John Emerson, who lived in Missouri, a slave state. Soon the doctor, his family, and his slaves moved to Illinois, a free state, then to Wisconsin, a free territory. Eventually, they all moved back to Missouri. The doctor died, and three years later, in 1843, Dred Scott sued Emerson's widow for his freedom. He said his former residence in a free state and territory made him free.

One Missouri court ruled in Scott's favor. He must have been thrilled at the ruling. But Scott's joy was short lived. In an appeal, the Missouri Supreme Court reversed the decision. Scott was not a free man after all.

Eventually the case was appealed to the U.S. Supreme Court. In 1857, Chief Justice Roger Taney ruled that Dred Scott could not bring a case in federal court because blacks were not citizens of the United States.

Taney could have stopped at that. But instead he went on to write that Congress could not establish any law that deprived a person of his property, and the word *property* included slaves. It was a victory for Southerners, but Taney's words angered abolitionists—people who were against slavery.

In 1860, Abraham Lincoln was nominated for president. A letter he wrote to a Southerner summed up what he and his political party believed. "You think slavery is right and should be extended; while we think slavery is wrong and ought to be restricted." If elected, he had no plan to abolish slavery in the states where it already existed, although he personally might have wanted to. He believed, however, that the national government had a right to keep slavery from spreading. The Southern states disagreed. They believed it was none of the national government's business. They vowed that if he were elected, they would **secede** from the Union.

Slavery then took a back seat to a bigger question. Did a state have a right to secede from the Union? South Carolina was the first state to test this question. It seceded in December 1860. Its declaration read, in part:

"We, therefore . . . have solemnly declared that the Union . . . between this State and the other States of North America, is dissolved . . . " South Carolina had "resumed her position among the nations of the world, as a separate and independent State."

After the South took Fort Sumter in 1861, the Civil War raged across the nation for four years. When the North was victorious two amendments were added to the Constitution: one which abolished slavery and another which prohibited states from taking away the rights provided by the Constitution.

Ten other states followed South Carolina's lead. They said the Union was just a league of friendship between independent states, and they had a right to withdraw if they wanted to.

But the North didn't agree. National supremacy over the states was clear to those who had signed the Constitution and those who had ratified it. Hadn't they debated this very issue over and over again? After all, the preamble to the Constitution read, "We the People . . . " not "We the States."

In his inaugural address, Lincoln affirmed that the states could not secede. The people could revolt and topple the government, or they could amend the Constitution and change the government, but they could not break away.

Lincoln was still interested in avoiding war, but when Southern troops took Fort Sumter in South Carolina, there was no turning back. The war went on for four years. The South surrendered on April 9, 1865. About a million men had been killed or were wounded to decide whether the

United States was to be a permanent Union or one that states could break away from at will. At the war's end, the question was answered. The Union was perpetual.

Now it was time to strengthen the Constitution once again. During the war, Lincoln had issued the Emancipation Proclamation that freed the South's slaves, but there had to be an amendment to the Constitution to end slavery permanently throughout the country. After the war, Congress proposed such an amendment and sent it to the states—including those that had tried to secede. The North had always and still did consider those states part of the country. On December 6, 1865, the 13th Amendment ending slavery became part of the Constitution.

The 14th Amendment in 1868 overturned the Dred Scott decision and made former slaves citizens. This amendment also did what James Madison's rejected amendment had tried to do: it prohibited the states from passing laws that violated the rights guaranteed to Americans by the U.S. Constitution.

The 15th Amendment said the right to vote could not be denied because of race or color. Almost another hundred years passed before the 24th Amendment prohibited other barriers to minorities' right to vote. Black men could vote after the 15th Amendment was passed, but there was another large group in the country that did not have the right to vote—women.

The women's **suffrage** movement began before the Civil War, when Elizabeth Cady Stanton and Lucretia Mott called a women's rights convention in Seneca Falls, New York, in 1848. The movement's goal was to gain suffrage, or the vote, for women. These suffragettes, as they were sometimes called, were disappointed when the 15th Amendment failed to include women specifically. After the Civil War, several states gave women the vote, but it was 1920 before the 19th Amendment guaranteed women's suffrage.

For years people wondered why young soldiers, such as this man in Vietnam, could fight for their country when they were 18 but not vote in elections. In 1971, the 26th Amendment to the Constitution was passed, and the voting age was successfully lowered from 21 to 18.

In 1924 an act of Congress granted citizenship to all Native Americans. But being a citizen didn't always mean all that it should. Some state laws continued to deny Indians the right to vote. It was 1948 before the federal courts overturned New Mexico and Arizona laws that prohibited American Indians from voting.

In 1971, voting rights were further extended. As early as 1954, President Eisenhower had made a plea to lower the voting age from 21 to 18. He had seen many young people sacrifice their lives for their country during World War II. He believed if people were old enough to fight and die for their country, they were certainly old enough to vote for its officials. Congress answered his request by introducing a constitutional amendment, but it failed. Nearly 20 years later, Congress again proposed an amendment to lower the voting age. This time it not only passed Congress, but it was ratified in an amazing 107 days. With that, the 26th Amendment gained the distinction of being ratified the fastest.

Since 1789, thousands of amendments have been proposed in Congress. Most of them were never passed on to the states for ratification. One of these failed proposals wanted to rename the country the United States of the Earth; another wanted to abolish the Senate—it was unlikely that senators would vote for that one!

Other proposed amendments have come close to being added to the Constitution. One of these in recent history was the Equal Rights Amendment, which Congress passed to the states for ratification in 1972. Opponents said that women had all the protection they needed under the Fifth and 14th Amendments. Those in favor of the proposed amendment disagreed, but the Equal Rights Amendment was ratified by only 35 of the required 38 states before its time limit for ratification expired. It did not become law. Since then, 16 states have put equal rights amendments in their state constitutions.

Other amendments will probably be added to the Constitution. Some may **repeal** earlier ones. The 21st Amendment repealed the 18th Amendment, which prohibited the manufacture and sale of intoxicating liquor in the United States. Whether to allow liquor to be manufactured and sold became a state or local issue, not a national one.

It is a tribute to those delegates to the Constitutional Convention that the document they wrote over 200 years ago has only been amended *27* times. It was a remarkable accomplishment, but they had the future on their minds. Delegate George Mason expressed awe at the idea of writing something that would have such an impact "upon the happiness or misery of millions yet unborn."

Like Alexander Hamilton, none of the delegates thought what they had written was perfect. They had practiced the art of compromise, and some came away from the convention feeling dissatisfied. They wondered if the country would soon dissolve in discord. But the delegates to the Constitutional Convention had done all that was expected of them and more. They had created a flexible document that could stretch to fit a changing nation. Its power did not come from the states, but "from the superior power of the people," according to James Madison. Although "the blessings of liberty for all people" have sometimes been slow in coming, Americans are still working to make the United States of America "a more perfect union."

Glossary

Amendments—Alterations or additions to a document.

Anti-Federalist—A person who was against a strong national government.

Appeal—To take a case to a higher court.

Articles—Distinct sections of writing, often numbered.

Civil war—A war between parts of one country.

Compromise—Agreement in which each side gives up a little.

Delegate—Representative.

Effigy—A representation of a hated person or thing.

Federalist—A person who favored a strong national government.

Infringe—Violate, cut into, compromise.

Preamble—Introduction.

Quorum—The number of people needed to conduct business.

Ratify—Accept, approve, endorse.

Repeal—Take back, cancel.

Secede—Withdraw.

Suffrage—Right to vote.

Veto—Reject, vote against.

Further Reading

Ben's Guide to the U.S. Government for Kids. Washington, D.C.:
Superintendent of Documents, 2000. http://bensguide.gpo.gov.

Bjornlund, Lydia D. *The U.S. Constitution: Blueprint for Democracy*.
San Diego, CA: Lucent Books, 1999.

DePauw, Linda Grant. *Founding Mothers: Women of America in the
Revolutionary Era*. New York: Houghton-Mifflin, 1975.

Fritz, Jean. *The Great Little Madison*. New York: G.P. Putnam's Sons,
1989.

——. *Shh! We're Writing the Constitution*. New York:
G.P. Putnam's Sons, 1992.

Hilton, Suzanne. *We the People: The Way We Were 1783–1793*.
Philadelphia: Westminster Press, 1981.

Jordan, Terry L. *The U.S. Constitution and Fascinating Facts About It*.
Napierville, IL: Oak Hill Publishing Co., 1999.

Morin, Isobel V. *Our Changing Constitution: How and Why We Have
Amended It*. Brookfield, CT: The Millbrook Press, 1998.

Index

ABOUT THE AUTHOR: Joan Banks has written over 100 articles and books for both children and adults. "One of my favorite parts of writing," she says, "is getting to find out about so many things." Recently, she has researched famous ghost stories, dinosaurs, groundhogs, and poison frogs. She especially likes to write historical books because she gets to learn about different times in history. Her two children are grown, so she lives on 13 acres in southwest Missouri with her husband, a dog, several cats, and a gaggle of geese.

SENIOR CONSULTING EDITOR Arthur M. Schlesinger, jr. is the leading American historian of our time. He won the Pulitzer Prize for his book *The Age of Jackson* (1945) and again for *A Thousand Days* (1965). This chronicle of the Kennedy Administration also won a National Book Award. Professor Schlesinger is the Albert Schweitzer Professor of the Humanities at the City University of New York, and he has been involved in several other Chelsea House projects, including the REVOLUTIONARY WAR LEADERS and COLONIAL LEADERS series.